Burgess-Carpenter Library
406 Butler
Columbia University
New York, N. Y. 10027

W9-ATS-880